The Story of
THE SUPREME COURT

By Kenneth Richards

Illustrations by Chuck Hamrick

CHILDRENS PRESS, CHICAGO

Library of Congress Catalog Card Number 74-1007

James Robinson tugged his collar up around his ears as he hurried along Broad Street. A cold February wind was blowing up from the harbor. There were not many people on the streets of New York on this cold Monday morning. Therefore it came as a surprise to Mr. Robinson when he found a small crowd standing by the old Royal Exchange Building at the corner of Water Street.

"What is going on here?" Mr. Robinson asked a man standing on the edge of the crowd. "Why is everyone waiting here on such a cold day?"

"Haven't you heard?" replied the man. "The new Supreme Court is opening today. It is to be the highest court in our nation. We want to attend the first session. It should be very impressive."

Just then the doors opened and a man stepped out and raised his hand for quiet. "The public is admitted to the court," he said, "but there must be absolute silence while the court is in session. You may enter now."

The crowd began to move quietly through the doors and up the stairs to a large room on the second floor. Mr. Robinson decided to follow. All of the wooden benches were quickly filled so he stood at the back of the room with several other people.

In a few moments a voice called "All rise!" Everyone stood up as the judges entered. When the three robed judges were seated at a large table, everyone sat down again.

"I recognize the judge in the middle," whispered Mr. Robinson to the man standing next to him. "He is Mr. John Jay of New York, but who are the others?"

"Mr. Jay is the Chief Justice," replied the man with a whisper. "The man with the wig is William Cushing of Massachusetts and the other is James Wilson of Pennsylvania."

The three judges were engaged in a low conversation for a few minutes and then Chief Justice Jay made an announcement.

"Justices Blair of Virginia, Iredell of North Carolina and Rutledge of South Carolina have been unavoidably delayed due to bad weather," he said. "Because we do not have a quorum of four judges, this court can conduct no business and therefore is adjourned until tomorrow afternoon at 1 o'clock."

With that, the people rose and the judges filed out.

The first meeting of the United States Supreme Court was over.

Mr. Robinson and the other spectators left the courtroom feeling a little disappointed. They had expected to see the court going about the business of handling legal cases. Yet all were aware that they had indeed witnessed a historic occasion. They knew that the Supreme Court was to play an important role in the government of their young nation.

Three years before, in 1787, a convention was held in Philadelphia for the purpose of rewriting the Articles of Confederation. The Articles had been the basis for a Federal government for the thirteen original states who had fought for and won their independence from Great Britain. But the Articles had proved to be too weak. If the United States were to become a strong, single nation, a new basis for central government had to be found. Fifty-five delegates from the various states worked for four months before they were able to present a plan for a "more perfect union" to the American people. It was called the Constitution.

Under the Constitution, the Federal government was to have three branches. Each branch was meant to be equal and independent. This system provided certain checks and balances to prevent any one branch from becoming too powerful. The Legislative branch (Congress) was to make the laws of the nation. The Executive branch, under the President, was to carry out the laws. The third branch, called the Judicial branch, was composed of the Supreme Court and other lesser courts as the Congress might decide were needed.

On March 4, 1789, the first Congress under the Constitution met in New York, the nation's temporary capital. In September, Congress passed the Federal Judiciary Act which provided for a Supreme Court consisting of a Chief Justice and five Associates. The same act also established three circuit courts, thirteen district courts, and the office of Attorney General. The Congress had now done its part in setting up the Judicial branch. The rest had to be done by the Executive branch.

Two days after the Judiciary Act was passed, President George Washington appointed the first Chief Justice, Mr. John Jay. Later he chose the five Associate Justices. In doing so he tried to be fair by selecting people from all sections of the country. Under the Constitution the Senate must approve the President's choices. They quickly confirmed the men President Washington had named, and a date was set for the opening session in New York.

The first six judges of the Supreme Court were well qualified for the high positions they had accepted.

All of them had been lawyers and three of them had been judges. And they had all helped to write the Constitution.

Courts are places of great and solemn dignity. There are few written rules that say how things are to be done. Mostly, the courts are guided by traditions passed along from generation to generation.

But, on February 1, 1790, the United States Supreme Court had no traditions. The only judicial system the judges had known was that of the mother country, England.

"The English judges have always worn robes," said Chief Justice Jay. "I think I will wear the robe I wore when I was a Doctor of Laws at Dublin University."

"The English judges also wear heavy, long wigs," said Judge Cushing. "I have such a wig. I will wear it and a robe too."

When Judge Cushing left the building after that first day of court, several children laughed and giggled at his great white wig. They had never seen such a thing before! Adults, too, stopped and stared in amazement. Judge Cushing decided that a wig had no place in an American courtroom, and he never wore it again.

The first session of the Supreme Court lasted only ten days. There were no cases to be heard and they spent their time admitting lawyers to the court. Before a lawyer can practice before the Supreme Court he must present his credentials. The Chief Justice must then accept the lawyer before he can be sworn in. Often, the lawyer will only appear before the court once in his lifetime. But it is a great honor to be allowed to practice law in the Supreme Court.

The Court met only once more in the Royal Exchange building. In 1791 Philadelphia, Pennsylvania, became the capital of the United States and the Court moved to that city. For their first session, they met in famous old Independence Hall where the Declaration of Independence had been signed in 1776. That summer, they moved to Old City Hall which was to be their home for ten years.

Meanwhile, the new capital city which was to be named Washington, D.C., was being built. The government moved from Philadelphia in 1800. President Adams moved into the new White House, and Congress moved into their new Capitol building. But no

the Capitol

one had provided for the Supreme Court. No building had been planned for the Judicial Branch. Instead, they were given a small room on the ground floor of the Capitol building.

When the Supreme Court met in Washington for the first time, in 1801, they had a new Chief Justice. His name was John Marshall. He was a Virginian and had been the Secretary of State under President John Adams. In later years Mr. Adams would say, "My gift of John Marshall to the people of the United States was the proudest act of my life."

Under the leadership of Chief Justice Marshall the Supreme Court became a strong force in the

the White House

national government. He believed deeply in our Constitution.

"We must always remember that our laws must be based on our Constitution," he said. "The decisions we make affect every home and every person in America."

The Court was scheduled to meet twice a year in Washington. Sometimes the sessions lasted a few weeks and other times only a few days. It depended upon how many cases had to be heard. But the Supreme Court sessions were not the only tasks the Justices had to perform. The various Judiciary Acts passed by the Congress provided for several Circuit Courts. Each Supreme Court judge was assigned to one.

Riding the circuit was a very tiring job. It meant traveling to many cities and towns in the areas assigned. At each place, the judge would preside over a court and hear whatever cases were brought before him. When all cases had been heard, the judge would move on to the next city. In the early days, before the railroads came, there were few good roads beyond the big eastern cities. The judges used stagecoaches as far as they could and sometimes boats. But many times they had to travel on horseback.

"On circuit duty in Maine and New Hampshire I spent fourteen days on a horse," complained one

judge. "I had to ride in heavy rain several days."

"Last winter, in western Pennsylvania, I was caught in a blizzard," said another. "After the storm ended I had to ride twenty-five miles through four feet of snow to reach my next court. We must ask the Congress to change the law that requires us to ride circuit."

Washington burns
—1814

But Congress is sometimes slow to act and it was many years before the law was changed.

In the meantime, the Court was given a permanent room below the Senate Chamber in the Capitol. They had been in this room only a few years when British troops arrived in August, 1814, and burned the Capitol, the White House, and other buildings. When the British left, the Court met for a while in a house on Pennsylvania Avenue. The Capitol building was finally rebuilt and the Court returned in 1819. In all, the Supreme Court was to make its home in the Capitol for 134 years.

Through the years there were few changes in the Supreme Court. In time it developed traditions of its own. When the great John Marshall died in 1835, Roger B. Taney was appointed Chief Justice. He set a precedent by being the first to wear long trousers under his robe. For years the Justices had worn knee breeches. By the time Abraham Lincoln became President of the United States, all the Supreme Court Justices wore simple black robes.

In 1860, the year Abraham Lincoln was elected President, the Court moved from their basement rooms to the handsome old Senate Chambers upstairs. Nine years later, the Circuit Court system was revised and the judges no longer had to ride the circuits. Instead, they held longer sessions in Washington, D.C.

Always, the Court acted with great and solemn dignity befitting the highest court in the land.

"We are very quiet there, but it is the quiet of a storm center," said Justice Oliver Wendell Holmes.

He meant that the Court often must settle cases about which there is much bitterness and anger on both sides. But the judges cannot take sides. They must decide the case quietly and fairly according to the laws of the United States.

For years, many people had urged the Congress to provide money for a Supreme Court Building. "As a separate and equal branch of the Federal government, surely the Court should have a building of its own," people said. At last a building commission was formed, headed by Chief Justice William H. Taft, the former President of the United States. Mr. Taft is the only person ever to hold the position of both Chief Executive and Chief Justice. In May, 1929, the commission received a design from architect Cass Gilbert. The plan, showing a handsome temple with simple dignified lines, was accepted. Congress provided nearly ten million dollars for the new building and a site was chosen near the Capitol.

Unhappily, Chief Justice Taft did not live to see the completion of his dream. He died in 1930 and was replaced as Chief Justice by Charles Evans Hughes.

It took many months of drawing, planning, and preparation before construction could begin. On October 13, 1932, President Herbert Hoover and Chief Justice Hughes laid the cornerstone for the new building. Nearly three years would pass before the building was finished.

"This must be a building of dignity and importance," said Mr. Gilbert. "We will build it with only the finest materials. We will use only the most perfect marble and stone, which alone will cost about three-million dollars."

The architects then began searching for just the

right marble. Giant stone quarries in Vermont sup-
plied some 25,000 perfect white slabs and blocks for
the outside walls. Sculptor James E. Fraser also re-
quired a great 250-ton slab from which to make his
handsome statues that stand beside the entrance.
Mr. Gilbert had designed four inner courtyards and
for their walls he chose fine-veined marble from
Georgia. For the inside walls he chose sparkling
white marble from Alabama.

The courtroom is the most important part of the
building and Mr. Gilbert had special plans for that.

"The courtroom will measure 82 feet by 90 feet,"
he said, "and I want the walls to be of the finest
'Ivory Vein' marble. We will have to get that from
Spain. I have also planned to have the ceiling sup-
ported by twenty-four marble columns. I want to use
a very special marble called 'Light Siena Old Con-
vent' which comes from a quarry in Italy."

Months passed as work on the new building pro-
ceeded carefully but steadily. Americans followed
the progress in their newspapers and in movie news-
reels. Some Americans thought it was wrong to spend
so much money on a building when so many people
were out of work. America was in the midst of the
great depression and many factories and businesses
had closed. But the building also gave Americans

faith in the future. The Supreme Court Building was designed to last for ages.

At last the job was finished and, on October 7, 1935, the Supreme Court met in its new building for the first time. Americans came from far and wide to see the beautiful new building standing opposite the East Front of the Capitol. Unfortunately, Mr. Gilbert did not live to see his building completed. He had died in 1934. But his building will be admired for centuries to come.

The judges were pleased as they toured the building for the first time. There was a carpentry shop where skilled cabinetmakers would work to keep the Court's furniture in good repair. There was an infirmary on the ground floor to provide medical care. There was also a complete print shop to publish official documents of the Court.

"What is in this room?" asked Justice Owen J. Roberts as he opened a door on the third floor. "Why! It is a gymnasium. Now we can exercise when we are not too busy."

"We can use the two large public conference rooms to meet with young law students and other groups," said Justice Louis D. Brandeis.

Continuing on their tour the Justices carefully inspected every room. They were pleased with the huge library which houses nearly 200,000 law books.

They nodded their heads in approval at the handsome, oak-paneled reading room with its great bronze chandeliers. As they walked down a white marble stairway, a Justice commented on how beautiful the staircase was. "Yes, it is beautiful indeed," replied Chief Justice Hughes. At the bottom he stopped and looked up through the stairway that spiraled upward for five floors. "But," he said with a chuckle, "I think I will ride the elevator UP!"

Never before had the Justices been provided with a place to read, study and work. They had always had to do it in their homes. In their new building, however, they found that each had been given a suite of three rooms called chambers. Each was also assigned a messenger, a secretary, and two law clerks. The law clerks are young law school graduates who help the Justices with their work. It is a great honor to be chosen as a law clerk for the Supreme Court.

The Chief Justice is assigned three law clerks and has larger chambers in which to work. He is also provided with a limousine and chauffeur.

Washington, D.C., is a city with many beautiful buildings, and the Supreme Court is one of the most beautiful of all. Many thousands of Americans every year come to visit the great institution which guards their rights under the Constitution. As they climb the broad marble steps, they leave the hustle and bustle of the city of Washington. Passing through the great bronze doors they seem to enter a whole new world. People move quietly about their business along the marbled halls and corridors. Everyone talks in low tones.

Visitors are admitted to the courtroom on a first-come-first-served basis when the Court is in session. The Court now sits from October to June. Those fortunate enough to get in, marvel at the handsome marble columns and the rich mahogany furniture. Heavy red curtains hang behind the judges' bench. Each of the nine black leather chairs is specially designed for each judge. Everyone is very quiet as they wait for the Court to begin.

A little before ten o'clock in the morning, two men appear and take seats at desks below the bench. They are dressed very formally. One is the Clerk of the Court. He has the important job of keeping the Court's records. He also swears in new attorneys after they are accepted by the Chief Justice.

The man seated at the other desk is the Supreme Court Marshal. It is the marshal's job to see that dignity and order are kept at all times. Visitors may not bring cameras into the courtroom and no one is allowed to make notes or to sketch pictures. The marshal is also in charge of the Court police. There

are thirty-two policemen and one policewoman assigned to the Court.

The lawyers who will present their cases to the Court are seated at two tables before the bench. There are seats at the side for others who may want to testify in the case or answer questions from the judges.

Sitting quietly behind the bench, are four court pages. They are high school boys, specially chosen for the job of serving the judges. The pages are there to deliver messages from the judges and run other errands. They attend the Capital Page School with other pages from the House of Representatives and Senate.

The scene is at last set. Everyone is waiting for the moment at exactly ten o'clock when the marshal bangs his gavel. Everyone stands. Then the marshal cries: "The Honorable, the Chief Justice and the Associate Justices of the Supreme Court of the United States!"

At that instant, all nine black-robed men step through the heavy red curtains behind the bench. They stand beside their chairs as the marshal cries out the traditional call: "Oyez! Oyez! Oyez! All persons having business before the Honorable, the Supreme Court of the United States, are admonished to draw near and give their attention, for the Court

is now sitting. God save the United States and this Honorable Court!"

The marshal bangs his gavel again and everyone is seated. The Supreme Court is officially in session.

And so, the work that began in the old Royal Exchange nearly two-hundred years ago, continues. During that time there have been nearly one-hundred different Justices who have served on the Supreme Court. They are appointed for life or until they resign or retire. Like the President and Vice-President, they can only be removed by impeachment.

The Court stands today as a monument to the American belief in freedom under law. The Court has no army to force us to do as it says. We have faith in their judgment and accept their rulings as final. Within their marbled halls, nine great men jealously guard the rights of the people under the Constitution. They work by their motto which is carved above the entrance to the Supreme Court Building. It reads:

"EQUAL JUSTICE UNDER LAW."

the Doorkeeper of
the Supreme Court

About the Author: Kenneth Richards began his writing career while he was in the U. S. Navy. And after his retirement from military service in 1966, he has continued to write. A New Englander by birth, he developed an early interest in American history. In 1963, Freedoms Foundation at Valley Forge awarded Mr. Richards the George Washington Honor Medal for a magazine article on the *Gettysburg Address*. Since then he has written many books for young people, including ten in the PEOPLE OF DESTINY series. Mr. Richards now lives in Pacific Grove, California, with his wife and four children.

About the Illustrator: Chuck Hamrick grew up in Memphis, Tennessee where his first formal art training was at the Memphis Academy of Art. Then after he earned a certificate in art and illustration from The Famous Artists School, Westport, Connecticut, he went to Baylor University, Waco, Texas, for four years of art study. His strong desire to become an illustrator was furthered when he received a full scholarship at the Art Center College of Design in Los Angeles, from which he was graduated with honors. Now he is one of Chicago's most talented young free-lance illustrators.